MW00718762

Serving the Master

Serving the Master

Devotional

Kay McDaniel

Book Editors:	Brandon Hyde
	Richard Heineman
Editorial Assistant:	Danielle Hyde
Copy Editor:	Ruth Lindsey
Inside Layout:	Richard Heineman
	Brandon Hyde
Photography/	
Image Aquisition:	Brandon Hyde

Library of Congress Catalogue Card Number: 2001099687

ISBN: 0-87148-4862

Copyright © 2002 by Pathway Press

Cleveland, TN 37311

All Rights Reserved

Printed in the United States of America

Dedication

I dedicate my first book in loving memory of

Dr. Cliff Schimmels
Dr. Janet Rahamut
Lorraine Jasso

To *Cliff,* who taught me the value of a story well told.
To *Janet,* who demonstrated by her life how to be
lovingly transparent to all of God's children.
To *Lorraine,* whose passion and love for life was a great role
model for the sufferings we all endure.

Table of Contents

Special Acknowledgments

I first want to thank my editor-in-chief,
The Holy Spirit.
I am grateful for the assistance of fellow Christians
who gave their support in various ways.
Without these individuals this book
would not have been accomplished.
Some of these people are
Brandon Hyde, Perspective;
Rich Heineman, Foil Pro;
Jonathon Dukes;
my family and many dear friends,
(Dr. Carbaugh, who is Matthew 25:36 in my life),
and Lee University.

Biography

Assistant Professor of Health
and Human Performance
Lee University

- **Professional Tennis**:
  Competed at Wimbledon and U.S. Open six times; French Open, three times; competed at Tournament of Champions; won professional tennis titles in singles and doubles; won British Airlines Concord Award for the "Fastest Serve in Women's Professional Tennis"; ranked top 30 in the world in professional tennis; competed against legendary players such as Billie Jean King, Chris Evert, Martina Navratilova and Steffi Graf.

- **Additional Experiences:**
  Christian and motivational speaker; writes weekly column for *Chattanooga Times-Free Press*; published writer; nominated to *Who's Who Among America's Teachers;* performs public relations for Lee University; actively involved in Emmaus and Chrysalis Community; received "Outstanding Achievement Award" by Louisiana Governor and Council on Physical Fitness and Sport; top five in the nation in racquetball.

- **Personal Experience:**
  I was diagnosed with systemic lupus and addison's disease in 1997; both are incurable. I contend with these chronic and progressive illnesses on a daily basis and walk in wholeness of health and victory because of the grace of Jesus Christ. Through this "thorn," God has richly blessed my development as a Christian warrior.

Foreword

Only a few times in life are you asked to do something that is not only an honor but a highlight of life; this is one of those times. Being pastor to Kay McDaniel has not only afforded me the opportunity to serve her but has also allowed me to be the recipient of the love and servanthood that come from someone whose passion is to be like her heavenly Father. Her life truly defines what Christianity is all about. Seldom is the beauty of life so exemplified from the inside out as Kay's life. No obstacle or hurdle has kept her from following and fulfilling God's will. Her beauty and Christlike nature have not been dampened by life's inequities, but she has used those unfair encounters to show her friends how to walk out their faith. Her fortitude and faithful perseverance have been a blessing to me personally as her pastor.

It is with great enthusiasm that I recommend this book, a glimpse of how this incredible woman sees and walks out life in Christ. Read it daily for inspiration and information on how to face life with full assurance in Him.

Kay is truly blessed and highly favored!

—Gary W. Sears
Kay's Pastor

As Kay's caregiver there are no words for the blessings God has given me. I was once asked if it was difficult to care for someone so sick. My instant reply is, "This is a privilege!" Who else can see Christ in the flesh on a daily basis? Her many diseases and struggles are what bring about the triumphant writings she now shares. I look forward to learning something new each day from this precious lady, and I'm sure you'll agree her wisdom and inspiration come directly from above. Enjoy the spiritual nuggets in this book as you learn to "Serve the Master."

—Dr. Sharon Carbaugh

Kay's Wall

The Wall

The red brick designing the outside library building of my elementary school was where it all happened. The many who knew me then would not be surprised that my special moments from school did not come from *within* the school but from where the bookracks were not located! The library's wall surrounded a cement parking lot and had faded yellow lines that secured space for vehicles. Positioned on this wall were two metal rustic pipes that ran vertically from the ground to the roof. I knew them well, for I scooted up them, like men on electrical poles, many times to find errant-hit tennis balls! This is where tennis came alive! This was my "field of dreams." One can never judge where dreams can be derived; with a little imagination they can come from mortar and stone!

Who would ever guess that this old library building held significance (especially because it was the back of the building); but to a skinny, runt-of-the-class girl, it was where it all began. It was "the wall"! It was at this place where I would pound hundreds of thousands of tennis balls. It made me improve because each ball would come back faster than I hit it! Here, I visualized becoming a professional tennis player. It was in my backyard neighborhood where I wanted to make the history books that were lodged in that building.

However, one never wins when playing against the wall! So I set goals. I would play countless mental games, verbally imagining the broadcast announcer saying," *It is 40-15 at Wimbledon, and Kay is playing against Chris Evert* [the # 1 player in the world at that time]. *The crowd is quiet knowing this is a big point. McDaniel is serving for match point . . .*"

Many goals were set and accomplished throughout the 15 years I frequented *the wall*. My first aspiration was to keep the ball low enough and to control it so I would not have to climb the poles to retrieve it! Later, I demanded more. The only way I could win the point would be to hit 500 backhands in a row and 400 forehands (I thought my backhand was weaker and needed more work). From the age of 11 until I was 26 I spent a multitude of hours alone at my wall. Whether I had just won a tournament or suffered a bad loss, I could be found the next day (sometimes that same night) at the wall—with a new goal to work toward. With every horizon was a new day and a new goal.

My dreams paid off! Billie Jean King, Chris Evert, Martina Navratilova, and Steffi Graf were formable opponents that I would later play against. But no one could match the wall.

"I Need Somethin' With Skin on It!"

Sarah lay awake in her room, afraid of what might be lurking in the dark. Her father came in several times to tell her that the Lord was with her; she had nothing to fear. Finally, in desperation she replied to her dad's theology, "I know, but I want somethin' that has skin on it!"

I can relate to Sarah. As a child I was positive the boogey-man was under my bed, too!

Isn't that the way we feel at times? We throw our hands up and declare, "I know You are here, God, but I'm scared! I can't seem to find my way out . . . Help!" All of us have asked the question in some form or another, "Where are You, God?"

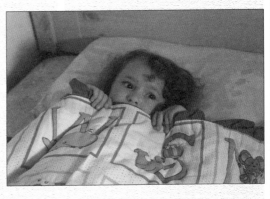

My raw feelings attached to those long summer days in 1991 are as vivid as a Polaroid snapshot. I was flattened on the bed not able to move more than a foot without my head spinning like a tightly woven top. Over and over, I would stand only to faint and fall to the ground. I was reduced to lying in bed like a mummy. There were no other options. The world seemed to pass me by without a hint of concern that I was not participating in its activities. Days and nights came and went without a word from God. *Did He pass by while I was sleeping and I just missed Him?*

The scantiness of my mobility was becoming a gut-wrenching reality. The depth of my physical depletion was exhausting my strength of spirit. The undercurrents of defeat were growing into white tides cresting and hitting the banks of my shore. My heart was desperate for a reply from God. My pallet was dry. My bones felt broken, crushed. Indeed, the virtue of long-suffering was being kneaded by suffering long!

During these times of despair, when there seems to be no movement in the camp by God, we can be encouraged by knowing God's directive to us: "Fear not, My child." It has been noted that at least 365 times in the Bible, God instructs us about fear—perhaps one warning for each day of the year! Because of this repetition, God must have known the pull fear would have upon our lives.

Jesus did not come to explain away suffering or remove it. He came to fill it with His presence.

Fear can stunt growth, isolate and paralyze. Fear unsettles us, causing foolish mistakes and shrouding sound judgment. However, take comfort, friend; wherever the peace of God resides, fear cannot inhabit.

May it be our daily prayer to rid fear's grip on our lives and thereby not suffer its consequences. In those frightful times God is with us. However, like Sarah, we need the assurance of "somethin' with skin on it."

Assurance in the Rock

Fear can clamp its dreadful talons into our lives and rob us of joy. It can darken our world by casting an ominous shadow over our heads. Fear can remove us from the scene and hinder the will of God. It can impede faith, steal dreams, and keep us from taking risks.

I was hiking with a friend who was an expert in outdoor activities. He wanted me to at least try repelling and scaling and seemed confident that I could do it. One day after a hike to the top, we arrived at the site where we began "my great adventure."

Repelling was a blast! Scaling the mountain, however, was another story. My friend demonstrated how it was done. His moves were catlike, and before I knew it he had scaled to the crest of the mountain. He had gone 75 feet straight up! Now, it was my turn . . . ugh! My spirit sank as quickly as he had ascended the mountain. He bellowed down to me how beautiful the scenery was, while my eyes only saw a massive boulder with minute cracks in it. Cotton-mouthed and wet-palmed I gazed up at this "landscape." When our eyes met, he saw mine were communicating, "I don't think so, Buster! It's just not going to work!"

My friend encouraged me as I mentally prepared for this expedition. After just a few feet, with terror gripping my heart, I grasped the edge of the mountain and yelled, "I can't do this!" I had no place to secure my toes (not to mention my foot or body!). He was not distressed—he didn't have a hint of doubt that I could climb this mountain. I had never experienced such penetrating, gut-wrenching fear, and as it entered my heart I lost the ability to see myself on top of the mountain.

For the next 30 minutes I pleaded my case, but he steadfastly coaxed me upward. Step by step I crept.

Finally, on top of the mountain I clutched my friend's arms and cried. As I peered thousands of yards down the steep mountain where we had parked the car, I embraced him tighter! Just thinking that I had been suspended in midair over such terrain by a single cord wrapped around my waist and hooked to a rather small tree trunk made me weep more!

Fortunately, one of my friends took a picture of this experience. Today, every time I see this photo I immediately exhale and silently think, *I did it!* I can still feel the tension of that moment and the exhilaration of success.

I not only climbed a mountain, but I also climbed atop the mountain of my own fear. It serves

Kay climbing the mountain of fear!

as a reference point, for when I hear of paralyzing fear, I immediately can relate to the plight of others with great compassion.

Don't let fear win! Dare to dream and climb your mountain. Fear can be overcome through assurance and trust in God. I gained assurance from knowing my friend believed in me.

Our Father believes in us, and we can place our confidence in God—the Rock of our salvation.

Seeing Beyond the Bar

Is hands were sweating as he grasped the towel to dry his grip before the next vault. He was waiting his turn in the competition.

> **The tournament:** National Junior Olympics
> **The event:** Pole vaulting
> **The athlete:** Michael Stone
> **The spectators:** 20,000

Michael's best career performance in the pole vault was below the height he was now staring at in this meet. The pole was set at 17 feet 3 inches. Michael was imagining himself flying over a two-story building in one leap. It was the moment, one shining moment, where all he had sacrificed and trained for was on the line.

Michael cleared the 17-foot bar while the crowd hollered with support. As quickly as he landed, Michael began to prepare for his next attempt at flying. He appeared oblivious of the fact he had just surpassed his personal best by 1 foot and the meet was down to the final two competitors.

When Michael accomplished 17 feet 2 inches and then 17 feet 4 inches, he again showed no emotion. His opponent missed the vault before him, and Michael now had the final jump. The next moments seemed turned into slow motion. The runway felt different and this briefly startled him. As his cleats grabbed the surface, it dawned on him that the bar was 9 inches higher than he had ever soared before. Anxiety began to fill his thoughts while his body began to quiver. His heart was pounding as if it were going to beat out of his body. He nervously wondered what he was going to do with these newfound feelings. He responded with a few deep breaths and shook his legs as if to literally shake off the tension.

A silence fell upon the crowd. Michael gently picked up the pole and began sprinting. Suddenly, the surface below him felt like the familiar country road he used to dream about. In his mind, he imagined rocks and chunks of dirt spraying as he pelted down the runway. When he took another deep breath, it happened. He began to fly. His take-off was effortless, and he seemed to float in the air. The air around him was the purest and freshest he had ever sensed. He heard only an indistinct hollow sound echoing his every move.

It was either the eruption of the people in the stands or the thump of his landing that brought Michael back to earth. While on his back, enveloped in the padding, he began to cry tears of pride. Michael was immediately swarmed with people hugging and congratulating him on this great accomplishment.

A little later that day he went on to clear 17 feet, 6 and a half inches. He not only surpassed his personal best by 9 and a half inches, but also set an International Junior Olympic record! Michael and those attending the meet will not forget that moment because *Michael was blind.*

A Decaying Message

"Fear is false evidence appearing real."

Gene Gilbert, a star British athlete, died in a dentist chair as the dentist was about to extract her tooth. When Gene was little, 30 years prior to this event, she had accompanied her mother to the dentist. Gene's mother was getting her tooth extracted when odd complications occurred, and Gene, a small child, saw her mother die in the dentist's chair. Fear shot into her heart, accompanied by the threatening thought that someday she too would die in a dentist's chair. It has been recently affirmed in research that negative imagery can be more powerful than positive imagery. It is harrowing to read about the grip fear had in Gilbert's life because this mental picture kept her from going to the dentist, regardless of her progressing dental problems.

At the core of fear is worry.

Finally, the pain in her tooth became so unbearable that the dentist came to her home to extract the tooth. Gene asked her minister and her family physician to stand by her side to provide comfort and assurance against her fears. At the moment the dentist put the bib around her neck and took out the instruments, Gene died. He had not touched the tooth! Fear became reality to Gilbert at just the sight of those instruments. The *London Daily Mirror*, which published the story, stated, "Gene Gilbert died of 30 years of thought!"

Fear can alter lifestyles and set up camp in our thoughts. If allowed, it will latch onto an event and distort our perspective.

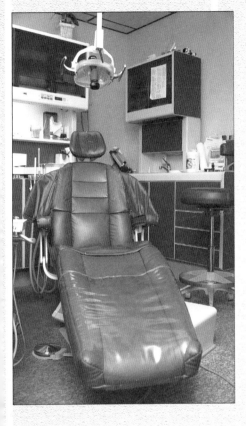

Fear will escort negativity through a small cracked place in a heart or mind. It will creep in the back door of a house we left unintentionally ajar. Fear is a major weapon employed by the Enemy, and it wins if it is allowed to defeat, discourage or destroy lives.

At the core of fear is worry. William A. Ward accurately depicted the war between faith and fear: "Worry is faith in the negative, trust in the unpleasant, assurance of disaster, and belief in defeat. . . . Worry is a magnet that attracts negative conditions; faith is a more powerful force that creates positive circumstances. . . . Worry is wasting today's time with yesterday's troubles."

Get the "tartar control" and wipe out any lasting decay so you can live in freedom, not fear.

"Fight truth decay: Read your Bible!"

Go Ahead, Laugh!

Did you know that on average 4-year-olds laugh 400 times a day? No wonder they're so much fun to be around! But the more solemn news is what transpires when we grow up. The typical adult laughs a mere 15 times a day! What a change in environment!

It's been noted that nothing reveals a person's character more than what makes him laugh. Indeed, laughter does break tension, strife and stress. What NBA player comes to mind when you think of a big, toothy smile? I thought so. Magic Johnson knew better than most that when we laugh we receive more than oxygen to the brain. Physiologically, laughter releases endorphins that energize us, increase our endurance, and act as a natural painkiller.

Mark McCormick, a leading sports entrepreneur and founder of IMG, believes laughter is good business: "Besides common sense, laughter is the most potent constructive force for defusing business tension."

Someone once said, "Laugh and the whole world laughs with you." Next time you make a blunder, instead of weeping, belt out, "That sure was a doozy!" You'll find others will cast aside criticism and opt to laugh with you. I have always found that if you laugh at yourself, you stop others from laughing at you! Mark Twain wrote, "The human race has only one really effective weapon, and that's laughter. The moment it arises, all our hardness yields, all our irritations and resentments slip away, and a sunny spirit takes their place."

Did you notice that kicking the trash can over didn't help much? Try laughing it off next time. Just maybe, he who laughs . . . will last!

A Titanic Gospel Message

Imagine this scene. A crewman of an ocean liner calls out the following message: "Come one, come all—get your ticket now! This ticket is invaluable and will be invalid if not accepted before the ship leaves the dock.

Make your reservations now to secure your spot on the ship. Reservations are going quickly . . . time is running out. Make your decision now so you can be aboard for the trip of your lifetime! The ship is at dock."

Each crew member bellows this warning while scurrying to get the remaining tickets sold. The ones already on board know that each person who walks onto this ship's plank will be changed after experiencing this voyage. However, decisions must be made now, for when the appointed time comes, there will be no turning back. This is *the* last call!

Our eternal ticket has already been purchased, and all we say is "Yes" to Jesus Christ. We must give God all our heart, mind, strength and soul(s), always believing in Him. Importantly, we must not let the ship depart without letting the world know that they have a right of passage. Jesus has paved the way for us, and our eternal stateroom is being prepared now. A mansion is being built uniquely for us. Our luggage need not be weighed, for there is nothing we can take with us. Our course has been clearly charted from the beginning. The final steps of obedience and responsiveness to the call from God are all we need.

You can feel it in the air; there is a restlessness among the ticketed passengers. Come one . . . come all . . . all aboard! The Captain has called your name.

"Hash—Mark It!"

There is a short sequestered line located on a tennis court that is no bigger than 3 inches. It is called the "hash mark." Players know it as the mark that divides the right side of the court (deuce) from the left side (ad). Even though it is quite minute in comparison to the other lines on the court, I have found it to be a significant visual to help control emotions while in competition.

Remember the last time you played for over an hour and the games were tied? The competitive juices were flowing and soon, someone would win the first set. Abruptly, you miss a "sitter." Another unforced error, and the momentum of the match could turn for your opponent.

Guess what? Another mess-up! Now, you are steamed and mentally unprepared to play the next point. Fuming over your last ridiculous mistake, you walk toward the back court to retrieve the ball. Your head shakes in frustration, not believing your pathetic attempt to execute a winner. A mere moment had passed, and another point and game had been tabulated, not in your favor either!

Nothing infuriates an athlete more than "unforced errors," or simply stupid shots! The worst defeat is the one inflicted on yourself. You kick yourself so much that your opponent's task is made easy. How can you avoid that self—imposed punishment? How do you stop the bleeding? One way is to "hash—mark it!"

The key is to maintain control of our emotions. If we don't, they tend to misfire and create more noise than the Fourth of July fireworks. If not properly taken care of, they can spark your opponent's confidence while extinguishing your own spirit. When it's needed, go ahead and express yourself! Take a moment to "unload" and redirect your emotions positively. Part of the learning process is allowing yourself to feel the sting for that misplaced shot. However, once you walk past the hash mark located dead center on the baseline, get over it. As you literally walk over the mark, strive to leave the past and its negative emotions behind by immediately focusing on the upcoming point. For some, that line comes much too quickly! If you are still too rattled to walk over the hash mark and start another point, buy yourself some time to "hash out" that last point. But once your foot lands near that hash mark, it's time to let it go! Forget those defeated feelings and face a new point, prepared for an opportunity to win.

Yes, it may be difficult to overlook those raw "inexcusable" errors, but train yourself to be "in the present." If you don't, the opponent is just waiting to grab a few more points from you.

Your weapon of choice? "Hash—mark it!"

The Clogged Heart

"But exhort one another daily, while it is called To day; lest any of you be hardened through the deceitfulness of sin" (*Hebrews 3:13*).

Every winter my pipes freeze, and this January was no different. After recent single-digit temperatures, we decided to inspect the external pipes surrounding the house. We were not sure which pipe was freezing, so we placed insulator cups around all of them. For a while, the problem was alleviated.

However, one chilly February morning, after only hot water came out in the shower, I realized the cold water was blocked. Impatiently, I got dressed and shuffled to check the pipes outside. All the outer pipes still had their covers over them, so where was the problem? After a long process of elimination, we tracked it down to three pipes inside the garage next to the water heater. They were located in a small pantry-like door, hidden from our view. It was a snug area, no bigger than a few inches. I used my hair dryer (not a recommended idea) in an attempt to thaw each pipe and found the last pipe was the culprit. Finally, all the pipes were clear and ready for use.

Physically, when our heart passages become obstructed, we need immediate medical help. If not, a hardening of the arteries occurs, which can be fatal. This is so similar to our spiritual lives because if we allow hurt to fester, it will harden into bitterness. Before long this process produces damaging anger, cynicism, mistrust, misguided remarks, depression and rebellion.

What's the answer? The key is to find the area where our "pipes" have been clogged! Something has caused our spirit to shut down, creating a weakness in our spiritual body.

Most likely it has been quietly simmering for days, weeks or months, but now it demands our attention. Do we recognize the warning signs? The cold hard truth is, if left unattended, the pipes will never clear themselves. The damage could erode and back up the system, causing a complete shutdown.

Spiritually, it is crucial that we ask the Holy Spirit's love, gentleness and forgiveness to melt any hardened area. If allowed, God will work at it until the area becomes like a brand- new pipe. It will be clean, clear, and ready for use. God will apply a balm ointment around the infected area so it can be restored.

When our pipeline is clogged, it is a "code blue" signal that something is wrong. It is a warning flag that must be heeded. Once action is taken, God's grace and mercy will dissolve the problem. He will be faithful to clear the passageway and remove the clog so we can pray and live effectively.

Billy Graham once said, "Sin is like ice in our pipes—our spiritual lives have been frozen. There is only one solution, and that is repentance to clear the blockage and restore the flow of the Holy Spirit."

Allow Jesus to be the "Liquid PlumR" of your pipeline to God!

"Oh, that you would hear him calling you
today and come to him!
Don't harden your hearts" (*Psalm 95:7, 8, TLB*).

The Master's Touch

When I gave my life to the Lord, the best metaphor depicting my spirit was a maverick. I was self-styled, contentious and unaffiliated. I was likened to a spirited horse which had never been caught, taught, disciplined or groomed. Some potential was inherent in this horse, but it was hidden because it had not been refined. At first, the horse did not welcome the forced boundaries, devices, and proximities. The process of putting on the horseshoes, bit, saddle, harness and stirrups was quite restraining to a horse used to running wild in open pastures. The horse was unaccustomed to such discipline; however, with much patience and tender care from the master, the horse learned to trust him. Slowly, the horse began to change and no longer ran with reckless abandon but let the master dictate the pace and route.

The horse desires solely to please her master. Yet, at times she still "kicks against the pricks," bucks, sputters and resists—especially when tired or hungry. There are moments when the horse still imposes a streak of independence and stubbornness and simply wants to go the old way, her way. She tends to forget that the road she once traveled will dry up and become desolate, and she would die. Some of the time this racehorse has blinders on her eyes and can only see what is ahead, blocking the beautiful landscape. The horse does not fully realize that around the bend in a green pasture is continuous running water, nourishing food, and a sheltered place to live. Thankfully, the master knows best and gently, yet sternly, steers the horse to these pastures.

It took the right master not to break the horse's spirit. It took the master's touch to train this horse. Those same qualities of willfulness, servility, and simplicity, if taught correctly, will set the horse apart. God's guiding our "spirited" ways so that, with training and in due season, we might shine in the Kentucky Derby Race called "Life."

This horse looks forward to reining with Jesus, just a bit!

Thank God for the Pain!

The morning of the citywide tennis camps (which I conduct each summer at Lee University) I got a phone call in the pro shop from, of all people, my doctor. He told me to get off the courts because the MRI revealed a herniated disc had caused a bone chip to be lodged in my spinal canal. The chip was pressing in on the nerves and causing my pain. It would have to be surgically removed immediately.

The next day I could not get out of bed, and I was in all practical terms stuck! God was with me. After I called a friend, an appointment was made with a top-notch neurosurgeon in another state. But . . . how was I going to get there when I could hardly see my toes, much less get up on them? God moved.

God gave me favor with the airline agent who secured a ticket the next day for $300 instead of the normal $850. Somehow, divinely and gingerly handled, I crept onto the Louisiana-bound plane, where I stood the entire trip from Tennessee. The place I "landed" was where I would literally stay for three nights; I did not move more than three feet. I was drugged with pain medication, muscle relaxer, and anti-inflammatory pills.

Nothing was working. I was beginning to lose motor abilities in my foot and leg. Finally, I saw the doctor and he performed surgery at 7 a.m. It was successful. However, because of the wait, I had incurred a "drop foot." This neurosurgeon who performed multiple back surgeries had not seen a patient recover from such a post-surgery syndrome. I could not lift my foot onto a curb; my strength had left me. I walked very stiffly and was stunned, wondering . . . would I ever be the same?

I had been a professional athlete, able to freely dictate my precise movements at beck and call. I commanded my body to perform supernatural feats on the tennis court, but it had never been pushed from these depths. I underwent rehabilitation every day, trying to restore my motor function and strength. Ever so slowly (as those who have agonized through this rehab process understand) my limbs began to "wake up." I gradually began to walk around the house and soon down the block. Eventually my tendons and muscles began to revive their elasticity. Within two years I was back to normal.

Meanwhile, during this challenging time, another person had a much greater tragedy occur in his life. The exact week I was facing such an unknown future, Christopher Reeve had fallen from an equestrian ride and was immediately paralyzed from the neck down. His life, literally, turned upside down and would never be the same. Whereas my problem was agonizing pain, "Superman's" obstacle was that he had no pain! He would never recover . . .

Upon reflection, during those months of back and body pain I found myself with renewed optimism and hope. Even though the suffering was difficult, I could at least feel my legs! Because of the many years of "buffeting my body," I had developed a high pain threshold. However, no discipline would be effective if all the neurons were not correctly connected.

It wasn't long before I began to be thankful that as the neurosurgeon routed his way to the trouble in my spinal canal, one tiny slip of his hand had not immobilized my ability to ever walk again! Without pain, my body's message center letting me know it is alive, my limbs would only be lifeless—dead.

I have never looked at pain the same. I learned a profound lesson that summer—thank God for the pain!

God's Siren

I had asked God to alert me whenever I sped in my car, something I do far too often. I need to be more conscious about it and, of course, I want to avoid a speeding ticket or a wreck. I seem to zip through life from meetings to classes to engagements, never mindful of speed limits. I need to form a habit and lifestyle of slowing down.

One particular afternoon I was flying to a class I teach at Lee University. I was pushing the accelerator, not wanting to be late—when I heard a loud siren blast behind me. Immediately feeling guilty, I slowed down. There was no police car nearby, yet the sound remained constant. I craned my head in all directions wondering if an ambulance was trying to whisk by and I was somehow deterring it. Again, no emergency vehicle! Seconds later it dawned on me.

Three years ago, my dad had given me a handy safety device for my car. It was a nifty lightweight protective gadget to use in case of car trouble at night or in a strange place. (My dad obviously felt this could occur with me behind the wheel!) I placed it in my car trunk and forgot about it.

This unique invention had several buttons to push depending on the situation. One button produced brilliant red and yellow flashing lights. Along with the lights came a shrill warning siren you would think could shatter glass.

This was the "siren" I heard. Sheepishly, I turned into the university parking lot with this awful piercing noise announcing my arrival. I turned off my car and opened the trunk. With all eyes glued on me, I silenced my blaring machine.

Suddenly, I remembered my previous prayer. I directly asked God to help me slow down while driving—without getting a ticket or being involved in a crash, He did!

"Coincidence is when God chooses
to remain anonymous."

David's Trust Factor

The trust factor in a Christian's spiritual life is the foundation of faith. Trust is that deep "knowingness" in the gut of one's heart. It is prompted by the Holy Spirit, who makes a strong witness to truth and intertwines with faith. This trust is supported by the belief that God is who He says He is in every situation. His nature and character cannot be changed or altered. It is trust in God that carries a Christian through life's storms. Trust is the substance that generates faith, and Scripture asserts that without faith it is impossible to please God.

 David, of Scripture, powerfully exercised these principles. In the face of a fierce battle, David inspected and evaluated the enemy (Philistines) and sized up his opponent (Goliath). At that point, David reflected on his own past experiences. He recalled the way "the Lord delivered [him] from the paw of the lion and the paw of the bear" (1 Samuel 17:37, *NIV*). These battles stoked his confidence. He declined to wear Saul's coat of armor that was specifically designed for warfare. Instead, his uniform of choice was a simple one that was familiar to him. It enabled David to trust God and not the armor during such a tumultuous time.

David was indignant with everyone sitting idly by and watching the opponent trample his team. Someone needed to fight because fear and intimidation had settled over the entire camp. David, the youngest of the brothers, garnered his strength by placing his complete trust in the living God. Isaiah 30:15 states, "In quietness and trust is your strength" (*NIV*). David was cognizant of what God could do, but it wasn't until he stepped out in trust and faith that he beheld the delivering power of God. Trusting in God is the Christian's offense and defense.

This trust is the glue that holds all things together in the midst of stress. John 14:1 declares, "Do not let your hearts be troubled. Trust in God" (*NIV*). Having done this, watch God demonstrate what He said He would do in your life!

> *Trust and*
> *obey for*
> *there is*
> *no other*
> *way for*
> *the warring*
> *Christian.*

Don't Bite Into That Apple—It's Rotten!

In the good ole' U.S.A., violent crimes occur every 17 seconds, murder every 29 minutes! Corruption is rampant in our streets: massive selling of drugs and consumption of alcohol, selling of bodies and selling of souls. There is no respect or regard for the other person. The drug dealer, madam, and gang leader are being used by Satan to destroy lives. At some point, these individuals decided not to resist further temptations; they compromised.

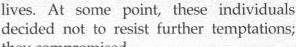
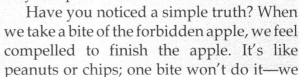

Have you noticed a simple truth? When we take a bite of the forbidden apple, we feel compelled to finish the apple. It's like peanuts or chips; one bite won't do it—we feel compelled to finish the bag! Sin has a habit of repeating itself. Its effects entrap vulnerable individuals and when faced with the reality of this condition, their spirits begin to squirm for freedom.

Panicked and under conviction—having innocent blood on their hands—they approach the dealer. They desperately want out, desiring a pardon. The drug dealers show their true colors during those moments, having no empathy for their plight or their souls. They sneer like the chief priests and elders did to Judas: "What is that to us? That's your responsibility" (Matthew 27:4, *NIV*).

Kids today, like Judas, feel there is no way out. They fall deeper into the dark pit of despair. Fear and depression take up permanent residence in their minds. Suicide seems to be the only door to exit this crushing pain—that's exactly what Judas thought!

In Acts 1:17, Peter said of Judas, "He was one of our number and shared in this ministry." Yet, Judas later died a violent death by his own hand. This Scripture says in effect,

"Hey, he was one of us! A fellow believer in Christ! A comrade in the faith! My brother . . . our brother!" Yet, Judas couldn't endure and chose to end his life.

Our world is inundated with individuals who are hurting, devastated by pain and loss. Many once knew Jesus, but fell into sin. They were deceived. The pain in their hearts dashed all hope and obscured their vision. They could not perceive any other route; there was no light at the end of their tunnel. It is up to us to point them back to God by showing them His redemptive power. After all, we are all sinners, and except for the grace of God, it would be us.

Remember, Christ left the 99 to go find the one who was in need. The father of the Prodigal Son wholeheartedly welcomed his lost boy back to the family. When anyone in our lives begins to demonstrate insecurities, become frightened or put up an overly strong front, you can know that the love of God is needed.

Christ is counting on us to reach our world. *If we don't, who will?*

"Have You Met Jesus?"

Have you ever been excited about someone meeting a special person? You just know they are going to hit it off; it's just a matter of coming together. If it were a blind date, the friend might say he or she is "just the right person for you!" All involved imagine an introduction that soon dives into a meaningful and lasting relationship.

Christ's disciples proclaimed Him to their families, towns, and even strangers. John 1:41, 42 notes that the first thing Andrew did was to find his brother Simon and tell him, "'We have found the Messiah.' And he brought him to Jesus."

When Jesus decided to leave for Galilee, He wanted Philip to follow Him. Philip was from the town of Bethsaida. In verses 45 and 46, Philip found Nathanael and enthusiastically told him, "We have found the one Moses wrote about in the Law, and about whom the prophets also wrote— Jesus of Nazareth, the son of Joseph." Nathanael grumbled, "Nazareth! Can anything good come from there?" Philip replied, "Come and see."

Jesus modeled the way we are to reach out to others, and the disciples tried to follow. On one occasion, Jesus was merely doing chores when He shared the gospel. In John 4:6, Jesus had just entered a new town along his journey. Tired from the trip, He stopped at a well to quench His thirst when a Samaritan woman came to draw water, and He struck up a conversation with her. The subject was natural—water. However, it turned into a supernatural moment when Jesus taught her about living water and eternal life. As a result, many of the Samaritans from the town came to believe in Him "because of the woman's testimony" (v. 39).

Jesus continually met with small groups and large gatherings, had meals with disciples and sinners. He despised religious tones and enjoyed talking about His Father and proclaiming the kingdom of God. He taught many truths by parables—simple stories.

Have you met Jesus? He is in town. Please . . . let me introduce you to Him.

Love Means Always Saying You're Sorry

The major theme from Erich Segal's best-selling book *Love Story*, written during the 1970s, was "Love means never having to say you're sorry." It was a real tearjerker! A dying woman and her husband contentedly assured each other during some emotionally distraught times that their love signified not needing to say, "I'm sorry." In relationships there can be a bonding that silently recognizes the other person is sorry for situations and conditions out of their control.

Other than "I love you," they may be the most influential words I will ever say.

However, I believe the most important and healing words anyone can say are, "I'm sorry." Those two words can bridge a gap, place ointment to a wound, and melt a hardened heart. Other than "I love you," they may be the most influential words I will ever say.

One of my desires I often fail to do is the expediency in replying, "I'm sorry." My hope is to be swift to forgive and forget. *God knows I have had plenty of practice in applying these words!* My primary objective every day is choosing to walk in forgiveness . . . as a lifestyle.

Also, it is essential that I acknowledge my wrong with no excuses following my apology. Have you ever noticed after asking someone for forgiveness you feel lighter, freer— maybe even more loving? It makes me wonder why we are not embracing every opportunity to apologize, since the results are so wonderful!

Scripture directs us to forgive each other (Ephesians 4:32). Then God will forgive our sin and will heal our land (2 Chronicles 7:14). Matthew 18:21 and 22 urges us to forgive and keep on forgiving, and verse 35 relates, "Forgive your brother from your heart." When we sincerely ask God and others to forgive us, we have pleased the heart of our heavenly Father.

God's love means always saying you're sorry.

"Who Put Salt in the Water?"

Imagine smelling the ocean, yet not being able to see or hear its movement! Nevertheless, Helen Keller dove into the cool water with wonder and excitement. Suddenly, without warning, her foot struck a rock, and the next instant a rush of water flooded over her head. She thrust with her hands to grasp some support, but all she found were globs of seaweed.

She panicked! Later she wrote about the incident, "The waves seemed to be playing a game with me and tossed me from one to another in their wild frolic." At last, as if the sea were weary of its new toy, it flung her back on the shore. Her teacher's arms clasped Helen and stilled her terror. After a few brief moments she regained her composure and simply replied inquisitively, "Who put *salt* in the water?"

Who would care about salt being in the water at such a time? Keller did not let this frightening moment scare her from enjoying the ocean. In fact, going to the ocean became one of her favorite and most frequented pastimes. She later noted, "I could never stay long enough on the shore."

Fear may reveal our frailties. Occasionally when we cannot see something, we fear it. The "fear of the unknown" can be disarming. For years I did not know I was fighting a disease because the symptoms did not remain constant. Many days harder to fight against this illness because it was "nameless" to me. Now, I fight a grittier battle because I am aware of this unknown. With God's enabling power we can get right back in the fight relying on God's stabilizing nature. He is always constant, true, certain, absolute, and will not be moved. You and I can count on Godamidst the swells of life's unknown seas. The next time fear splashes us in the face, may we respond, "Who put salt in the water?"

A Millionaire's Mentality

"If you want to know what God thinks of money, you have only to look at those to whom He gives it."

Much to my surprise, there are not as many millionaires in the world as I had presumed. Even though a millionaire today is not worth nearly as much as in the past, a millionaire is still a millionaire!

In a quick glance at the book *The Millionaire Next Door,* a typical millionaire is truly akin to the average "person next door." Those neighbors we would never suspect as even being middle class are quietly stashing away wads of money.

Most millionaires were "C" students who felt inferior and knew they needed to get better—quickly! So, they raised their shirtsleeves above their elbows and got dirty ... working. They honed a laborious work ethic, year after year, and paired it with common sense and wisdom against idleness and frivolous living. As proof of their "commonality," many millionaires own merely two credit cards (Sears and Penney's) and one in 10 own a Ford. Eighty-five percent of millionaires are first generation—they earned it themselves (signifying it was not "old" money or inheritance). The millionaire's motto is simple: "Live below your means, be frugal, and know where to invest your money."

Can you recognize the typical Christian? Is he who he seems to be? You know, the person whose checkbook reveals the heart of God. The sad truth is that only

> *The sad truth is that only 3 percent of Christians tithe.*

3 percent of Christians tithe. Yet the Bible has much to say about money. Did you know that 16 of the 38 parables were concerned with how to handle money? In fact, one in 10 verses (288 in all) deals directly with finances. According to Howard Dayton Jr., Scripture offers 500 verses on prayer, fewer than 500 verses on faith, yet more than 2,000 verses on money and its possessions!

The Christian is that person who can be found amidst sinners ministering Jesus Christ. Christians have studied God's principles regarding finances and are busy investing their lives away. Time, gifts, talents, career and money are freely and joyfully given for the advancement of the kingdom of God.

After all, the Christian's motto is "My life is not my own; it is God's and all glory goes to the One I serve." Is that you?

Have you ever found yourself remarking, "You always . . ." or I would never . . .?" We might be stunned to notice how frequently we begin a sentence with a boast, exaggeration, pretense or excuse. When it occurs, a reality check is necessary to rearrange our thoughts from the flesh to the spirit of God.

Some statements with bad beginnings might reveal pockets of pride hidden in our hearts. For example, have you ever said, "If the decision were left up to me, I would have done ..."? Have you ever scornfully rebuked someone by commenting to a friend, "I would never do what she did because ... "? Comparing ourselves to others is usually a bad fit simply because we do not know the full story or haven't carried their burden. It is worth remembering that we have never walked in their shoes, and if we had . . . we probably would have done worse!

Have sharp words stabbed your heart and made you feel justified in retorting, "I have every right to get back at him for doing me that way—he was wrong and he knows it. How dare he smugly think he's better than everyone else!" We often hear a prideful beginning such as, "I could have done a better job than she without any training. It doesn't take a rocket scientist to figure it out! What was she thinking"?

Comparing ourselves to others is usually a bad fit.

Maybe over the years individuals have rubbed your mistakes back in your face by announcing, "I told you so!" Even if it's true, those biting words, coupled with a condescending tone, can raise the hair on your nape. Temptation often follows, urging you to rebel even further just to spite them and their words! Now you're in a fine place, aren't you?

If this isn't you, perhaps you are hostile when people have different ideas than yours, provoking a haughty attitude—especially when you know your way is the best.

Clearly, the best pronouncement on these prideful moments is in Romans 12:3: "Do not think of yourself more highly than you ought, but rather think of yourself with sober judgment, in accordance with the measure of faith God has given you."

"If you make a mistake and do not correct it,
you've made another mistake."

The Doll

Helen Keller's aunt made her a doll out of towels. It was shapeless with no nose, mouth, ears or eyes. Helen would later recount, "Curiously enough, the absence of eyes struck me more than all the other defects put together. I pointed this out to everybody with provoking persistency, but no one seemed equal to the task of providing the doll with eyes."

Over the years this same doll had been pulled and yanked, thrown and beaten. One significant day Helen remarked, "I dashed it upon the floor. I was keenly delighted when I felt the fragments of the broken doll at my feet. Neither sorrow nor regret followed my passionate outburst. I had not loved that doll."

Minutes after this tantrum, Helen and Anne Sullivan (her teacher) would venture to the well house where her understanding would change. She "read" and understood the word w—a—t—e—r which Anne signed into Helen's hand as the water poured from the pump over her hand.

At that precise hour, Helen for the first time understood language and a whole new world opened up to her. Helen's thoughts of that poignant moment read: "Thus I came up out of Egypt and stood before Sinai, and a power divine touched my spirit and gave it sight. And from the sacred mountain I heard a voice which said, 'Knowledge is love and light and vision.' "

Reentering the house, she remembered the broken doll. She tried vainly to put all the pieces back together when a second revelation occurred to her. She wrote, "My eyes filled with tears, for I realized what I had done, and for the first time I felt repentance and sorrow."

Helen learned many words that day, but none so important as *repentance*. God had set her free. Although her sight was never restored, her spirit was. She pondered that earlier day and penned, "It would have been difficult to find a happier child than I . . . for the first time I longed for a new day to come." Helen Keller had discovered hope. Even without her sight, she quickly became an avid "pupil" of life. She never stopped learning.

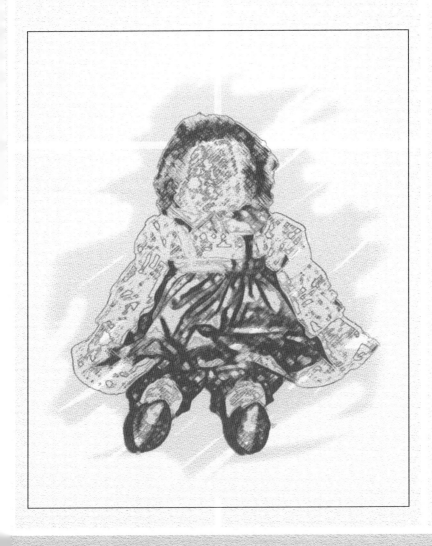

Today, What Would Your Obituary Read?

A lady had a particularly scrumptious dish that everyone salivated over when they ate it. When anyone asked her what the specific ingredients were in this delicious salad, she consistently answered, "Over my dead body!" When she died, guess what was carved on her headstone? *Yep, her recipe!*

Luci Swindoll had a friend who told her she had used up so many sick days she would have to *phone in dead!*

> *We are writing our epitaph one day at a time.*

Seriously, long before Alfred Nobel fathered the Nobel Prize, he invented the modern form of dynamite. In fact, few know he founded a financially successful dynamite factory. Some years later, Alfred's brother died. Due to a reporter's mistake, the local newspaper published the obituary of Alfred Nobel instead of his dead brother. The following morning Alfred read his own obituary. *What a wake-up call that would be!*

Line by line, Alfred read his obituary. It described him as the man who invented dynamite so powerful it could instantly reduce a tall building to debris. However, reading his life story "shook" Alfred's world. He began to reflect on the meaning of his life. Nobel questioned, did he want to be remembered for a destructive invention or for a cause more noble?

Immediately, he began to revise his obituary—thus a philanthropist was born.

What if you were alive tomorrow to read your obituary in the local paper? Would you be satisfied with the few statements regarding your life's purpose? If not, what would you change? If you could compose a different obituary, what would it say?

Many individuals who enter midlife or retirement years ponder this question, wishing to live again without regrets. What would your funeral oration note; how would your epitaph read? *Would you right yesterday's wrong and forget today's hurt? What would Jesus say about your life up to now?*

It is not too early or late to finish this statement: "If I were to start life over again, I would . . ." When you and I die, it will be too late to change the way we lived. Now is the time to change and align ourselves with the unique plan and will of God. Each one of us has a distinct purpose in life. What is your destiny?

Remember, we are writing our epitaph one day at a time. Let's immediately begin to live differently than our last moment, for Christ's sake.

No Excuses!

> "A man may make mistakes, but he isn't a failure until he starts blaming someone else."
> ~ *John Wooden* ~

I read a *Sports Illustrated* article written by Rick Reilly titled "Need an Excuse? Take It From the Pros." Reilly wrote about big leaguers denying and justifying their wrongdoings. A defenseman for the Anaheim Mighty Ducks winced, "I didn't do anything wrong"—after swearing at a referee, smashing his stick, nearly hitting an official, and getting a game misconduct penalty. A former Boston Red Sox player, after refusing to take a Breathalyzer test during an arrest for drunken driving, and after failing eight sobriety tests when he couldn't get past the *M* to recite the alphabet, explained through his lawyer, "I was taking allergy medication."

An NFL coach remarked to the press, "Don't forget I'm 60 years old." That was to explain how he could have forgotten he was carrying a loaded revolver when he passed through an airport security check.

A 1998 U.S. Olympic hockey player said in reply to the ransacking of three rooms by U.S. players at the Olympic Village in Nagano, Japan. "They were flimsy, anyway. All you had to do was sit on them, and they'd break."

Athletes are not the only ones who find alibis for their mistakes. All of us are guilty of tagging on after our sins, "But . . . " Wrong is wrong because it's a wrong. Scripture notes that when we know what is right and do not do it, we sin (see James 4:17). Martin Luther King Jr. said, "The time is always right to do what is right."

The great evangelist Charles Finney remarked, "We should swallow our excuses, nullify all self-justification, and squelch all rationalizations. Merely state, 'I'm sorry' and be done with it. Godly sorrow leads to repentance unto salvation without regret."

We, as Christians, must not seek excuses but repentance. Of course, this is much easier said than done. To those who participate at all levels of sport and in life, are you adding a "but" when you fail?

Kay, are you striving to do what is right? . . . No excuses!

The "V-Team"

"Carry each other's burdens,
and in this way you will fulfill the law of Christ."
(*Galatians 6:2*).

"A friend should bear his friend's infirmities."
~ *Shakespeare* ~

W*e are forever blood sisters!* As a child, did you ever say these words with all sincerity and meaning as a covenant pact with your friend? Do you recall the seriousness of this solemn declaration representing your "stick-together-like-glue" relationship? Why, you even sealed this vow with a prick to the finger and blended your blood with hers. At that moment, you're convinced nothing could separate the two of you; you were bonded forever—that said it all!

When a friend asks us to pray, how do we choose to carry her burden? Do we get militant by drawing our weapons for battle? Do we get "down and dirty" as the oxen when pulling shared weight on our shoulders? Or maybe we're more like an unbending archer who takes the arrow back and targets the bull's eye through accurate Scripture-based prayer?

What picture best depicts the mode by which you "carry burdens" for others? Unfortunately, most of us become like a scared fighter shadowboxing and flailing in the wind.

We could learn invaluable lessons from observing the mannerisms of geese. After all, as Christians we are also flock members, of another order. Geese instinctively garner a certain style of "burden carrying" when they fly north for the summer or south for the winter. It is known as the "V-formation." When the head goose of this "V" gets weary, it falls back and another goose takes the leadership position.

Further, the remaining geese fly precisely behind the leader where the wind is least resistant. This is so aerodynamic that cyclists and runners have taken the same strategy to "draft" off one another to save energy efficiency for the team's long race.

Another trait worthy of imitating is, that when one goose becomes ill or hurt, it does not leave the "V" alone; two other members of the "V-Team" fall out of formation and follow the wounded goose. After landing, the healthy geese tend to the frail one until it is either able to fly or dies. Moreover, they will put themselves in jeopardy when predators seek to overwhelm their weakened friend. The detached two or three geese then wait for another group of geese to fly overhead, and they join them, increasing their safety and flying effectiveness.

Yep, if we learn to flock together like birds of a feather, then we too could soar!

> "Our duty is not to see through one another,
>   but to see one another through."

"For With God Nothing Shall Be Impossible"

Examples From Scripture

- Was Goliath too sizable for the living God in David?

- Was the erection of the wall too laborious for a praying Nehemiah?

- Was the fiery furnace too consuming for servants of the Most High God in Shadrach, Meshach and Abednego?

- Was the den of lions too intimidating for a trusting Daniel?

- Was the parting of the Red Sea or the forging through the arid desert too unperformable for the delivering power of God in Moses?

- Was the building of a 450-foot long, 75-foot wide, and 45-foot high ark too formidable for a righteous Noah?

- Were 90 years of age and a barren womb too impossible for God to birth a promised child in Sarah?

- Was a call from God—at age 75—that mandated he leave his country, people and household, and sacrifice his only son, too difficult for an obedient Abraham?

- Did Peter's denials of Christ banish him from anointedly testifying about his Lord?

- Were the thorn in his flesh, intense suffering, and repeated persecutions a stumbling block for a persevering Paul?

- Was Jesus' garment out of reach for the outstretched arms of a desperate woman?

- Were prison and chains too confining for Paul and Silas to sing praises to God?

- Was sickness, to the point of death, too incurable for the faith of the centurion?

- Were the background and past transgressions of the sinful woman at the well too unforgivable for God?

- Are the strategies of Satan, worldly entanglements, and fleshly tendencies greater than the One who abides within us?

- Were the Crucifixion and burial too insurmountable for our risen King?

Is not heaven waiting for those who have
not seen and yet believe?

Teamwork

"The body is a unit, though it is made up of many parts; and though all its parts are many, they form one body."

The word *team* stands for **T**ogether **E**veryone **A**ccomplishes **M**ore! Isn't that a truth worth repeating? If you ask any great running back or volleyball player the secret of his/her success, one will most likely respond: "I had a great front line blocking for me," or "Our setters kept us in control."

A good question to help maintain team perspective is "Who passed the ball to you when you scored?" Former First Lady Hillary Clinton titled her book *It Takes a Village,* noting the whole town is needed to make a difference in a child's life. Jesus Christ first initiated this concept; we have just missed the message! Similarly, it takes the work of every member on a sports team to have ultimate success. Every strong team knows the value of an individual's defined role to accomplish the team goal.

Rowing is an excellent example of the significance of teamwork. It is a team sport of six, requiring each individual to perform specific duties. Accuracy and speed are essential in order to make the canoe-like boat glide effectively. Each participant has a distinct job. The first athlete is called the stoker, and the last is the steersman. The stoker makes the calls while the steersman's responsibility is to "know the water." He is the only team member who looks around during the race. Athletes in positions three and four provide the "engine" or power for the boat.

In practice, many teams will do everything together, even to the point of literally being tied together to learn to function as a unit. *The more they are "one," the more efficient and powerful they will glide through the water.*

Someone once wrote this simple phrase: "Team Unity: Think in Sync."

No other Scripture text better reveals this truth than 1 Corinthians 12:12: "The body is a unit, though it is made up of many parts; and though all its parts are many, they form one body."

Athletes are summer missionaries

Tennis team 'serves' the Lord

By CARISSA LONAS

During the summer months many Lee College students are involved in various forms of ministry. Some travel with choirs, some on mission trips, and many work in churches in their own community. In July one team of workers minister on our campus courts—tennis courts, that is.

Three years ago Kay McDaniel, head coach of the women's tennis team and former professional tennis player, began holding free tennis camps for kids in the Cleveland community. With the help of Paul Conn, president of the college, McDaniel was able to structure the camp as a community outreach.

The camps are open to boys and girls between the ages of 8 and 18. The camps are broken into two age groups, and they also separate boys and girls. Each

Head coach Kay McDaniel serves up tennis and testimonies to Cleveland's kids free of charge.

team members, she integrates the message of the gospel into her instruction. For the first 15 minutes of each day, the kids hear a testi... and her women's ... ate days speak... day of the week ... ch kid a chance ... Savior.

...as received an ...ositive response ...d parents. She ...ng to see kids ...d those that al... are encouraged ... they hear."

McDaniel their children can't stop talking about the camps. Some have commended McDaniel for using her tennis skills to convey the gospel. Said one parent, "The kids hear about Jesus all the time from parents and youth pastors, but they are excited to hear the message connected to something like sports."

CHATTANOOGA FREE PRESS   ★★★★   SPO

Lupus Gives Way To God And Kay

Kay McDaniel was in Nashville for the state racquetball tournament this weekend, winning the women's A Division in a romp and reaching the semifinals in women's open.

After defeating nationally 10th-ranked Sheila Collins 15-12, 15-10, 15-11, McDaniel lost 11-9 in a deciding third game to Ellor Morgan recently moved from Kentucky where she was ranked No. 1.

It normally has no big... Daniel, although at 36... high women's tennis... tate to journey com... racquetball, she was... recognized name on... tion bar for several... winning the round of 16... the quarterfinals at the... she logs in her original... Wimbledon and the...

... ince out-blazed Mar... lava for the Concorde... invited for the fastest... nee's tennis.

devastated, fearing a virtual end to her tennis and golf activity. Lupus and the sun just don't mix, she was warned.

But Kay, buoyed by the newfound religious convictions that led her to Lee, remained a ray of brightness to all who met her. She denied a wig and joined a softball team and still remained far more active than many people — and far more outspoken about God's greatness.

Even when she became very sick, debilitated for months by infection, her radiance was infectious.

"She has really been a fighter. I know she has worked a lot of times when she wasn't physically up to it," Lee vice president and athletic director Henry Smith recently observed. "But her spirits have always been very high.

"She is a great lady."

And her fight is apparently being won.

Hear her own testimony.

"When you're in good health, everything seems great, and I've been in good health for a year and a half now. I'm the strongest I've been in six or seven years," she said this past week.

"I truly believe I'm walking in...

FEELING GOOD: Kay McDaniel, Lee College women's tennis coach and former WTA pro, feels God's healing in her battle with lupus.

She also teaches seven classes, runs the much-used DeVos Tennis Center, coaches a team toward the upper echelons of the NAIA and goes to school herself. Since she's been at Lee, she's earned a B.S. degree in Biblical education and is just four credit hours short of a master's in sports science from the U.S. Sports

The Anger Issue

"Anger is only one letter short of danger."

If you can't just "get over it," perhaps the core problem is the confidence issue, not an angry personality. Are you overly confident? Do you expect too little or too much of yourself or others?

Do you make excuses for your behavior, always blaming others for your failure? Consciously or inadvertently, do you perceive certain situations as a threat—to who you are and your belief system? Are insecurities hidden in your life that have not been addressed?

What about pride? Who do you think you are? Michael Jordan? Cal Ripken Jr.? Doc Anderson? Mia Hamm? Matthew? Mark? Luke? John?

Assess why you act or react the way you do. Take inventory. Just as important as when the athlete dresses for a game and has his entire gear ready to go, the athlete needs to take note of his mental equipment. Is any excess baggage hanging around your thinking? If so, trim the fat! Do others a favor and shape up! Initiate corrections wherever isolated pockets of distorted thinking have occurred. Address them before they become distracting patterns! If you don't learn to harness your temper for yourself, do it for others! Realize that your anger affects not only your performance but the behavior, attitudes and climate of others as well.

Also consider this: Do others want to accept Jesus Christ into their lives based on your life? Does your passion for excellence in character dominate your ability to control your tantrums? Are you disciplined by the Holy Spirit and yielded to the fruit of the Spirit? Can people tell the difference between you and an unbeliever? Where's the difference?

Before you "lose it" next time, think of the other person and the trail of people you have impacted! Are you leaving a destructive or constructive path for others to follow?

What kind of influence would you have on someone's daughter, mother or grandson? *Get a life! It's not just about you.*

"Just Live It!"

Most true elite athletes will not brag about their greatness. Yes, egotism abounds in sports, but the real "greats" do not toot their own horns. Legendary athletes let their skills speak for them. They merely allow their bat, lacrosse stick or basketball to do the talking. In fact, champions are usually the first to say, "My bad" after a missed shot, taking all the blame on themselves. They do not feel a great compulsion or need to discuss their spectacular achievements. They let others do that as they "just do it."

An actor does not flaunt his starring roles to others; he lets the ticket sales at the box office do that for him. The politician does not need to tell us who he is; we already know by his actions. A person operating with the gift of mercy does not need to remind us of this gift because she exudes it. Mercy pours from her pores; even the air around her is filled with merciful aroma!

A mature Christian does not call attention to himself by boasting of his spirituality. An authentic Christian simply lives Christ. He strives to do God's commands on a daily basis, moment by moment. The committed Christian is firm in who he is in Christ Jesus; his identity is wrapped up in God. His confidence is not derived from himself, but from the heart—where God lives!

As I see it, Paul strongly addressed our weaknesses. In Scripture, Saul (who became Paul) did not boast about his mightiness. On the contrary, look up 2 Corinthians 11 and 12 and you will find Paul only talked about his faults and shortcomings. Why? So that God would be glorified and honored through verifying Scripture, "His strength is made perfect in our weakness" (see 12:9). Paul understood that his inner strength came solely from God, not from anything he said or did.

Paul even bragged about his shortcomings, stating in 2 Corinthians 11:30, "I will boast of the things that show my my weakness" and in 2 Corinthians 12:9, "Therefore I will boast all the more gladly about my weaknesses, so that Christ's power may rest on me."

Let us evict our arrogant attitudes and humbly yet confidently "just live it."

"I have been driven many times to my knees by the overwhelming conviction that I had nowhere to go.
My own wisdom, and that of all about me,
seemed insufficient for the day."
~ *Abraham Lincoln* ~

"Oh ... My Word!"

"Your words are windows to your heart."

I knew I had entered this conversation late, but I couldn't believe my ears! The chatter was heated and intense, and when I heard words that implied a significant suggestion of wrongdoing, I quickly tried to ignore its possible meaning.

Yet, a few nods and concerned frown lines came with, "He shot himself!" The other person quickly replied, "But he didn't have a gun."

I quivered and could feel my body tighten. I wondered, *Maybe I'm too sensitive because yesterday in one of my classes I spoke on suicide.* This conversation had my mind in a quandary.

Hastily I interjected, "Shot?" They responded, "Yeah. . . ." I paused and sighed deeply, my head dropping. Their eyes widened.

"He got shot, you know . . . 'headed'!" (For those just as ignorant as me, this is the lingo for being stapled or tattooed.) Their conversation carried on not missing a beat, while my heartbeat slowly returned to normal.

What if I had walked away after the phrase "He shot himself"? How much damage could I have caused?

If you are not convinced of the power of perception, watch a large crowd work this game. Start by passing a short phrase that contains a couple of catchy buzzwords and whisper it to the person next to you. Ask individuals to repeat what they hear to the person next to them until everyone has heard. After the game is completed, question the middle and end person in the group what he or she heard. Then tell everyone your original phrase. It might be revealing how awful our listening skills are and how clumsily we dispatch information! Isn't it amazing how we can malign a mere sentence! But it happens every day, which is exactly how rumors start.

We simply listen with halfhearted, lazy ears! We perceive, presume, and misconstrue words! Couple this with a tendency to believe the worst in people and suddenly . . . we have a full-blown scandal! Instead, let's try this mentality:

"You can never speak a kind word too soon, for you never know how soon . . . is too late."

"He shot himself . . . but he didn't have a gun."

"How High, God?"

A coach fervently declared to the athlete, "Jump!" The champion athlete instantly responded, "How high?" At a board meeting the CEO explained to the administrators what was needed to further their corporate success, and

Quick obedience is the correct answer to a command from God.

they replied, "Consider it done." A Christian relayed a prayer request concerning a family member and before he finished the statement, *the pastor was praying.*

One year a lanky All-American came to practice with a full beard. When the press asked about it, the player strongly stated, "It's my right!" His coach, John Wooden, heard this and remarked, "That's good, Bill.

I admire people who have strong beliefs and stick by them, I really do. We're going to miss you." Bill Walton shaved it right then and there. Today, Walton still calls "Coach" once a week. Wooden, who is over 90 years of age, coached UCLA for 40 years and tallied 38 NCAA, titles once said, "Discipline yourself, and others won't need to."

Quick obedience is the correct answer to a command from God. The illustration found in Luke 7:1-10 is one of my favorites regarding the spirit behind obedience. A centurion (a military man) was greatly worried about a servant who was gravely ill. He heard Jesus was nearby and sent a group of fellows with a specific request of Him. Once these men found Jesus, they pled earnestly for Him to travel to this dying servant . . . I can hear them saying, "You would love this guy, Jesus. He's your kind of man. He has passionately built our local church, and he loves his nation. Please, come quickly; he needs you."

Jesus followed the men to the house but was abruptly halted by another set of friends from the centurion. When the centurion saw Jesus approaching his home, he humbly recognized Christ as being a man in authority. He understood the relationship between a master and a servant, and at that moment he must have slapped his hand on his forehead and said, "What am I thinking? Jesus is a busy man! He is about His Father's business, so I must tell my men that all Jesus needs to do is just . . . say the word and my servant will be healed."

Once this message was delivered from the centurion, it melted the heart of God. Jesus turned to the crowd and replied, "I tell you, I have not found such great faith in all of Israel." (And among that group were His disciples—just like you and me.)

The other day I was shuffling paperwork around on the kitchen counter, trying to select which bill to pay first. As I finished writing the last check, my eyes caught a glimpse of several organizations I had wanted to financially support for quite a while. However, I was acutely aware of my dwindling bank account. At that moment, while reading about a particular association, I suddenly heard a television commercial blurt information about that very organization!

With a wide grin and a cackle, I looked up and responded, "I'm jumping, God. How much?"

> "Greatness in the kingdom of God
> is measured in terms of obedience."

It's the Extra Stuff!

Have you noticed that committed people do the extra stuff . . . well? They go the extra mile with a smile, and you can recognize them by their work ethic. They are running while you are whining. They hang out longer in practice ("just 'cause"), and when they practice, they are intently focused on the job at hand. These individuals or teams make small daily sacrifices, constantly trying to improve on some facet of their game and settling for nothing short of excellence.

A chief scout for one of the NHL teams expressed it quite adequately: "The main thing is that the player is willing to give that little extra when it's needed . . . 10 minutes more in practice. He takes responsibility to prepare himself to give that little more. . . . When he is down, he gives a little more . . . even when he might be dead tired. . . . This separates the good hockey player from the great hockey player." Does Wayne Gretsky come to mind?

The mediocre Christian might rejoice sometimes, while the committed Christian "rejoices always." Some average believers may pray when in need, but the steadfast Christian will "pray without ceasing." A common follower of Christ will give thanks in the good times; however, the entrusted believer will "give thanks in everything." The lukewarm Christian desires to stay away from evil, but the God-fearing warrior will "abstain from every form of evil."

Basketball legend Pat Riley said it best: "There are only two options regarding commitment. You're either IN or you're OUT. There's no such thing in life as in-between." Of course, the originator of this viewpoint was Jesus. We are either hot or cold in our faith commitment in Christ; there is no in-between.

Comebacks

"Every setback is an opportunity for a comeback!"

"Rudy! Rudy! Rudy!" was echoing from the famed stadium at Notre Dame University. The chants were for an unknown player who had dreamed since an early age of playing football at just such a prestigious institution. Rudy was from a small town and the first of 14 children from a poor steel factory family. His desire to attend and play football for Notre Dame was considered "foolish," given his financial background and poor GPA. Rudy finished third in his class— third from the bottom. He was a "D" student that graduated from high school with a 1.77 grade point average. Rudy lacked elite football experience and was only 5 feet 9 inches and a mere 190 pounds (a linebacker today averages 250 to 300 pounds!).

Rudy enrolled at a community college to raise his grade point, and eight years after he graduated from high school, at

the age of 26, he became a registered student at Notre Dame. However, getting on the football team was another story. In his spare time he worked on maintaining the field, keeping it immaculate for the players but never playing on it. Although beaten up and bruised after each practice, Rudy eventually made the team. He never played one down at Notre Dame until the last seconds of the last game during his final year. When the coach signaled him to run onto the field, the crowd was cheering, "Rudy! Rudy!" with his teammates spearheading the chants. He made a tackle, and the game was over.

Were all his work, ridicule, and sacrifice worth one play? Yes, because of the character this process built into Rudy and the example he set for all who watched him. Let us persevere for the honor to fulfill our dreams. "Whatever your hand finds to do, do it with all your might" (Ecclesiastes 9:10).

"Stay on track when on a comeback!"

Disguised Blessings

Having just endured another episode of sickness by the grace and power of God, I thought a few words with a heavenly perspective would be appropriate.

I have experienced the richest of blessings many, many times in my life. I deserve none of them, yet God continues to bestow an abundance of gifts to my life. Indeed, His promises are "yea and amen." It has been easy to open my arms broadly and embrace these blessings from God.

Receiving God's provision has never been difficult. However, when times of trial and suffering come my way, I am not nearly as quick to wholeheartedly accept them! Hardships are, at times, agonizingly painful. They can severely wound our physical body or attack the deep recesses of our heart. During these fragile moments my insecurities and fears rise to the surface with volcanic force. They shout at me like a flashing neon sign. Now, I recognize my utter weakness within the magnitude of God's strength. My limitations are visibly apparent. But that simply means the possibilities for God to perform miracles are noticeable and plentiful. When I fall short of the mark, God is just beginning to orchestrate His majestic handiwork in my life. When hope disappears and despair rushes in the back door of my soul, God walks on the front of peace and contentment. He either offers a way of escape, strength to endure, victory in the face of defeat, or beauty amidst the ashes.

These perilous times drive me closer to God. One of my most frequent prayers to God is that I would see my world through the eyes of faith—to have my Father's eyes. My goal is to earnestly maintain eternal perspectives as I journey through the earth. I believe perspective and attitude are the most crucial pieces of equipment during times of battle.

They provide a way to peek my head above the troubling

waters. An otter swimming in the sea frequently lifts its head up for air and receives a broader perspective of where it is going. I, too, must be able to visualize and capture the bigger, more significant picture during life's interludes. Otherwise, I will miss the point, obscure the painting, and not fully learn the eternal life lessons fashioned by God. Then, the Master Teacher must find another way, at another time, to open His message to His pupil.

So the trials and sufferings I have encountered can be deemed as precious blessings and treasures from my Father. Each one has been filtered through nail-pierced hands. God is intimately aware of each test He has enabled me to endure. He walked to the cross for me, and He walks with me now as I take up my cross. Many times I have just endured the cross and felt it was a victory in itself. Yet, I would later discover hidden pearls—a less restless soul, deeper inner strength, and assurance that God is at work controlling all events for this believer's good. During these moments, like none other, God works into my soul virtues of Himself that I could not possibly acquire without Him.

Much like a chef working with yeast, God kneads His virtues into me that I may conform to His image. He stretches, pulls and tugs away at the excesses of my carnality. He is in pursuit of those places within me that are obstacles and hindrances to His plan. This process is His answer to my familiar prayer: "I want to be more like Jesus by being transformed into His image." Then, and only then, can I make a difference in my world for Christ's sake. The way He answers my prayers may not be comforting and pleasing at the time. However, He hears my cries and knows perfectly well how to bring abundant fruit from my lamentations.

Indeed, trials and sufferings are responses to prayer. Paul

is a powerful example of one who endured multiple hardships, yet received bountiful grace from God. Like a good father, God is pained to see disappointments come upon His children; however, He understands the whole, not the part. If trials have their perfect way, they will bring about His desired result.

These stopovers along life's journey may be the necessary guidance that keeps me walking down the straight and narrow path to heaven. Without them, would I be tempted to wander like a sheep looking for its shepherd? Virtues received—passion for Christ and compassion for others, patience and long-suffering, understanding and insight, brokenness and yieldedness—may be the essential fuel that energizes me to accurately point others to God and proclaim the kingdom of God.

Through the disguised blessings, I will be fulfilling the mission of the gospel of Christ. I want to stand for what Christ died for.

So be it in me, Lord. So be it.

"Life's Not Just, So Adjust!"

"It takes suffering to widen the soul."
~ *Billy Graham* ~

We don't live long before we can conclude, "Life's not fair!" Silently, our heart churns like a washing machine struggling to rinse out the unfairness life throws our way. But sometimes the stained spots just won't come out!

We bristle, "What about our rights as believers of God? Don't Christians receive 'special privileges'? If they do, why is life so hard?"

Some people amply shrug their shoulders, sigh with a touch of sarcasm under their breath, and say, "Que ser'a ser'a"—Whatever will be will be." In modern lingo, that means, "Whatever, God!"

Does it seem the things we desperately want to see change, don't, and that which we wish wouldn't happen, does? Sometimes life's significant thorns stubbornly stay in the same place. Paul felt these sentiments too. In anguished words of disgust, throughout the New Testament he begged for fewer thorns.

However, somewhere between these two appreciable differences (things that change and those that stay the same) lies a clear and level perspective. Our question is How do we balance the scales before the wrong side slams down to the ground . . . before we become bitter, not better?

It's rather simple. Take a long, strong glance outside yourself, and you will soon awaken to the realization of "how good ya got it!"

From time to time each of us desperately needs an "attitude adjustment." Remember when you wrecked your car or had the unfortunate occasion of someone's doing it for you? Afterward, the first thing required was "an estimate"— an appraisal for the value of the car. While the damage to your car was being assessed, every spot was exposed to this Sherlock Holmes of the insurance industry! Dents that occurred when your 16-year-old drove the car suddenly glare for attention. Scratches from loaded arms banging bags in or out of the car, and even hailstones contributed by Mother Nature are all keenly noticed by the inspector.

After three years of impatiently reducing my medication one tiny gram at a time, we were anticipating a breakthrough from the doctors. Medications necessary for life-threatening diseases can sometimes be more difficult than the disease. I was hopeful there would be a better way to live.

"I determined to be grateful..."

After making three different trips, eight hours each time, to a famous research hospital, we were posturing ourselves for the good news. My heart was beating rapidly, ready for an anticipated solution.

After the doctors examined my ever-increasing file, they popped my hopes with the sharp facts: "Kay, you cannot be a candidate for experimental treatment because the harsh reality is your body is wasting away." I must live on high dosages of several medicines for any hope of a quality life—even to sustain life.

In my heart I felt it, my family and friends saw it, and the most prestigious doctors had now confirmed it. That familiar quote, "Lord, grant me the serenity to accept the things I cannot change, courage to change the things I can, and wisdom to know the difference" became agonizingly real! They were not just pretty words floating on the pages of a lacy devotion book. They now had to be my prayer.

We all are tested and need to learn that whatever life deals, there is a way to adjust! After a sad heart for a few weeks, I knew soon it would be time to readjust.

My perspective changed. I determined to be grateful that I even had medicine to continue my life. Slowly but surely, my attitude began to transform as I allowed God to "do an attitude adjustment" on my thinking. I wouldn't be alive today without the intervention of medicine.

I have found over and over again that God is God and He is sovereign. Friend, we can trust the results of our prayers when they fall into the all-knowing will of our Father.

In fact, in His arms "Que ser'a ser'a"—"whatever will be will be"—is perfect!

Missing the Point

"Too many churchgoers are singing 'Standing on the Promises' when all we are doing is sittingon the premises."

I vividly remember a specific time in 1994 when I disappointed God. I broke my Father's heart. What could be worse than wounding God?

My close friend, Quanita, and I had been conversing on the phone for years as she lived in Mississippi and I in Tennessee. That past year had been particularly hard for her; she had contracted cancer. Her arduous bout with chemotherapy left her with a dejected spirit and in need of seeing an old familiar friend.

While visiting my family in Louisiana during Christmas, Quanita called and wondered if I could come to see her. It was a wonderful idea! I ended our conversation affirming that I would work out the details and see her soon.

I simply blew it.

The days passed quickly, and without warning I realized my designated return to Tennessee was in two days. After wrestling over the 10 hours to drive round-trip to visit Quanita, I rationalized that it would be too difficult to make the trip at that time. I called her and apologized for having to turn down her gracious invitation. I anxiously set a definite date to see her the following summer.

Four months later I heard the terrible news. My dear, close friend had died. I deeply regretted my shallow decision not to visit her that day. God, knowing her remaining days were numbered, had given me an opportunity to see my friend one last time. . . . He knew how much it would have meant. I simply blew it. To this day, I still have her name in my address book with stained teardrops smudging the area around it. It's a reminder of God's "divine appointments" in our lives.

It serves as a point of conviction to me, like when the disciples couldn't stay awake to "watch and pray" for their Lord.

Remember the scene? It was the hour of destiny—the moment Christ needed the disciples "to be there" for Him. Scripture says, "His soul was overwhelmed with sorrow—even to the point of death" (see Matthew 26:38). There was no relief in sight. At that moment He knelt as He talked to His Father, who had never left Him.

After Christ had prayed, He returned to the disciples. Instead of pounding on the door of the throne room of heaven on Christ's behalf, they were snoring away among the rocks without a care in the world! Christ must have been deeply frustrated and hurt at His disciples ,who missed the point entirely. Why didn't they realize what was about to occur? Not even the brutal physical pain He was about to experience on the cross could match the agonizing anguish Christ felt in His spirit.

I am not alone in missing the mark. The disciples disappointed Christ, misinterpreted His teachings and power, doubted and denied Him, and simply lacked faith. These original disciples did not set out to wound Christ. But they did. I never intended to miss such a precious moment with my friend. But I did.

As Christians we often fall short of the mark; however, this makes the gift of God's grace even more valuable. When our shortcomings are glaringly visible, God's grace is gently magnified. At these moments we become acutely aware of our humanity and dependency on God. In humility and through failure, I am learning to seize each moment and not miss the point.

One Point at a Time

One of my most memorable athletic feats occurred not in professional tennis but in college. I was a junior representing the Bengal Tigers of LSU in the season—ending National Championships. Players from California and Florida easily ruled the rankings. I was seeded 12th and was facing a formidable foe in the third round. She was an amateur but had played in professional tournaments and was ranked in the top 40 in the world.

To place a proper perspective on the moment for this Louisiana gal, I had never seen a professional player in person or even been a fan in the stands of a professional tournament until that summer at the U.S. Open. My opponent's talent intimidated me: She served better, was more powerful, and exuded superior experience and confidence.

Not long after the match began, I found myself down 6-2, 5-0 and 40-love. She was serving for the match—three times over! I was as far down as a player can get. One slight miss hit and the match was over. I clearly remember my only thought at that desperate moment was to get the ball back just one more time—no matter what. I somehow won the following sequence of points, broke her serve for the first time in the match and won my first game in the second set. Of course, this didn't mean much because I was still down 6-2, 5-1, but I had a glimmer of hope. Keeping the same strategy, the points, though close, fell my way.

The momentum slowly started shifting. Like a hound dog on a hunting trip, I began to sniff a weakness. As I began to accumulate the games, I was still in a jam. We entered "sudden death" (when the games are tied 6-6, a mini-game is played.) I found myself down triple match point again! I scraped by, won those points, and the second set. For the first time since we walked on the court, the score was even. I went on to win the third set 6-4 and advanced to the quarter finals to play the #3 seed in the tournament.

I have played over 25 years of tennis and have never been down to that extreme in a match. It was like playing in the World Series, and your team is down 3-0 in games. It's the 9th inning of Game 4, you're down six runs with two outs. You stand in the box with two strikes against you. The possibility of coming back is microscopic. The fans have already left the stadium, the vendors are counting their money, and the manager is looking down, not to see the impending final out.

However, this is the moment you imagined as a kid growing up—the great comeback! It is "being down but not out."

Even though no one believes you can, you do.

Even though no one believes you can, you do. It's the American dream. It's the substance of which small businesses are made. It is the "pick me up" a person looks back on years later to help him restore hope and belief. It's the little red engine that thought it could . . . and did. With God as our conductor, believing is achieving.

Just take it one point at a time.

"You Can Always Come Home"

It was a hot, muggy, late evening in Baton Rouge. It had been a long day; we were weary from packing, moving boxes and traveling. I was an LSU student. My parents and I were eating cheeseburgers at an unfamiliar restaurant watching buckets of rain pour down. Seventy-two hours earlier I had no idea I would be going to college, let alone a huge university on the far side of the state.

Already I was late. School had started three weeks earlier while I was trying to decide whether or not to play on the professional tennis circuit. To top it off, I was assigned to the only dorm available—the oldest dorm on campus, affectionately called the "Dungeon." Of course, my room was buried in the basement with no windows or air-conditioning. (Keep in mind, this was mid-August, and a person can sweat just thinking about the temperature and humidity in the bayou state at that time of year!)

Mom!

As the rain poured, so did my tears. I was already lonely and questioning the sanity of my decision. As my family was saying goodbye, my mom's departing words were endearing, needed and unforgettable. She sensed that my fear of the unknown was gaining ground over the excitement of new challenges. She tenderly said, "Kay, you can always come home."

Whenever I had moments of apprehension (they were plentiful!), my heart remembered those words. They became an emotional safety net to catch my falls when I lacked confidence and needed support. Just knowing the net was underneath gave me the courage to face the fears of a new life.

A few years ago a commercial came on TV that reinforced this message. It began with a zoomed picture of an authentic country cabin in a rural landscape. The only light in the area came from the full moon. The crickets and frogs provided constant background music. In the rear of the house the beginnings of the local news could be vaguely heard.

A man dressed in old, ragged overalls opened the squeaky door and shuffled to the edge of the porch. Dark ominous clouds were quickly approaching, accompanied by severe winds. Random lightning bolted and grumbling thunder crashed. Yet, there was an eerie stillness on the porch as if the old man were in the eye of the storm. Looking deep into the dense woods, the man calmly whistled a familiar "come home" tune to an unseen dog. As the rain pelted down, an old Irish setter shuffled in with just a hint of damp fur. The scene slowly faded, and these words softly appeared on the screen with a serene voice wooing, "Channel 12, a place to come home to."

No matter how difficult life may become, as Christians we always have a place to call home. Indeed, we are strangers only passing through, awaiting our promised land and eternal home—heaven.

Until we walk into that glorious place, do you hear our Father on Heaven's porch calling us, telling us we can always come home?

Going a Step Further

"The measure of who we are is
what we do with what we have."
~Vince Lombardi~

Wilma Rudolph had just sped her way past the other competitors to help her team win the 100-meter relay race at the 1960 Olympics. Immediately, this hero was swarmed by people wanting snapshots and autographs. She had hurdled her way over poverty, prejudice and polio. Wilma had plenty of company being the 20th of 23 children in her family (she would later involve herself in an underprivileged children's foundation). She was a four-time all-state basketball star from Clarksville, Tennessee.

But it was running that gave her the most joy. When the Games began, few knew she had a severely sprained ankle. This seemed slight compared to her childhood days when she was 11 and wore a leg brace because of polio. However, the next day Rudolph would be the first American woman to win three track-and-field gold medals.

Amidst all the clamoring and vying for her attention that day, Wilma untied her running shoes and signed her name on each of them. She reached across the crowd to give them to a small shy fan.

Her medals were earned at the finish line, but to me, her true success was measured by her gesture to the young lad. It was a "shoe-in" victory for the future of the sport.

That pair of shoes will be hard to fill, especially coming from one who was born in Bethlehem . . . Tennessee.

"Stop! Don't Lose That Lesson!"

Many times when we lose the *battle* we ultimately win the war— if we don't lose the crucial life message on the battlefield. For the expectant individual, there is always a lesson to be learned, but it takes a keen eye and open heart.

Many coaches will attest that winning is a product of centering concentration, and the reward goes *not* to the team that was great but to the one who made the fewest errors. It's not the gathering of winning ways that contributes to success but the management of mistakes and the mental alertness necessary for efficient recovery.

 Did you know more than 50 percent of all CEO's of *Fortune 500* companies had C or C- averages in college? That nearly 75 percent of all U.S. presidents were in the bottom half of their school classes? And that more than 50 percent of all millionaire entrepreneurs never finished college?

Teddy Roosevelt said, "He who makes no mistakes, makes no progress." The first time I went snow skiing, I found the most difficult challenge was the simplest task— getting up after I had fallen! Over and over again I wearily picked my sore body up from the side of the mountain. My ski suit was drenched when I finished that day, proving I certainly had ample opportunities to get better at this task. Even though I did not like falling, it was an inherent part of learning how to ski! Also, if I had stayed on the snow with "all fours looking at heaven," the park officials would have closed the mountain on me.

How long will it take us to acknowledge that the hidden nugget in life is how we learn from our failures? We seem to be blind toward the meaning of failure. It doesn't take an uneducated Einstein to educate the world.

DisAbled?

Winston Churchill said, "You can tell when you're on the road to success when it's all uphill." Did you know that over one-fourth of the greatest world shapers had a severe physical handicap and three fourths of these came from extreme limitations in their background? Disability hits the common folk too. Some statistics show over 30 percent of all workers will be incapacitated for at least a 90-day period before they reach 65 years of age.

Marla Runyan is one of the best runners in America evidenced by her five gold medals in the 1992 and 1996 Paralympics. At 9 years of age she was diagnosed with Stargardt's disease, a degenerative condition of the retina. Runyan is legally blind. However, she raced and finished first against *able*-bodied contenders at the Pan American Game and finished in 10th place (of the 1,500 contenders) at the 1999 world championships. Her invisible focus is clearly depicted in this statement about running: "I always know where the finish line is. It's at the end of the straightaway."

I am inspired by individuals like Marla Runyan, John Milton, Helen Keller, and Ludwig Von Beethoven, who overcame their disabilities and turned them around to abilities. Neither lack of hearing nor sight stopped them from running the race of their lives. In fact, some of Beethoven's greatest music, including his Ninth Symphony, was performed after he was completely deaf.

Theodore Roosevelt said it well, "There has never yet been a person in history who led a life of ease whose name is worth remembering."

How Are You Aging?

"We are happier in many ways when we are old than
when we are young; The young sow wild oats.
The old grow sage."
~ *Winston Churchill* ~

Guess what population is the fastest-growing segment in the U.S.? *People 85+!* Americans age 65 and over out-number teenagers. Currently, there are over 61,000 members of the 100+ club (*centenarians*) and by 2020, there will be 214,000.

It is documented that a French and an African woman lived 122 and 125 years of age respectively.

Even some fish live to be 140, and behold the pine tree, for it can live 4,800 years—the oldest living organism!

Whew! It can be tiring just thinking about living such a drawn-out time period. However, this data is helpful, provided our bodies hold up and endure to the end.

It is one of my goals to maintain quality fitness so that I can participate in the Senior Olympics (it's sooner than I would like to think—I need to start now). These Games were held not long ago in our area with the winners seeing stiffer competition when representing our state at the National Senior Games.

I endeavor to smash the racquetball around. There are four walls to this game; certainly I can hit one of them! I am currently biking 10 miles every other day so I won't collapse before the finish line, and I look forward to throwing a pass to my partner for a key lay-up on the courts.

Experts say the way we age depends less on who we are (genetics) than on how we live. Most of the physical decline that older people suffer stems not from age but from simple disuse!

Take heart, it's never too late. Look at Frank Havens, who at 27 won an Olympic gold medal in the 10,000-meter canoe race. At age 62, he was still competing and beat his gold medal time by one minute!

David Costill, captain of the Ohio University men's swim team in 1957, turned in top times for the 200-yard individual medley and the 200-yard freestyle. After age 46, he had actually improved these times, and by age 53, he was faster in every event he had competed in at age 20!

Al Oerter was the four-time Olympic discus gold medalist in the 1956, 1960, 1964 and 1968 Games. He won the 1968 Olympics at the age of 32. When Oerter was in his 40s, he held *masters* records in the discus that were better than his Olympic throws!

Health scientists are discovering that often accompanying longevity is a strong faith in God. It is imperative that we believe so we can not only "age gracefully" but better yet "age actively."

Above- "Par Excellence"

"Success hinges upon a passion for excellence."
~ *President John F. Kennedy* ~

Abrilliant example of integrity occurred in 1994 when Davis Love was playing superb golf in the Western Open. In the middle of this second round, he moved his marker on the green to place it away from another player's putting line. A couple of holes later, his conscience pulled at him. Had he put the marker back in its original position? He couldn't remember. So he summoned the official over and called a one-stroke penalty on himself.

He didn't have to do it. No one would have known. Ironically, that one stroke caused him to miss the cut and get knocked out of the tournament. That one penalty was an expensive one.

To make things worse, by year's end, Love was $590 short of automatically qualifying for the next year's premier Masters Tournament. The only way to get into this event would be to win a tournament. A reporter asked him how much it would bother him if he missed the Masters because he had called a one-stroke penalty on himself. Love replied, "That's not the question. The real question is, How would I feel if I cheated to get in?"

This story gets even better! With just one week, the last possible opportunity to enter a tournament before the Masters, Love won a tournament in New Orleans, qualifying for golf's finest event. How did he score? You will "love" the finish; Davis Love was runner-up at the Masters, earning some pocket change, $237,000.

The "D" Word

The Design of Discouragement

Once upon a time, Satan, growing weary and old, decided it was time to retire from active work. He offered all his devilish inventory of tools for sale to the highest bidders.

At the time of the auction, he laid all his wares in a neatly arranged row: defeat, despair, depression, discontent, deception, disillusionment, doubt, and denial. Each was plainly marked based on its effectiveness.

In the front was one ungainly piece that was priced surprisingly high: *discouragement*. It cost 10 times more than any other evil weapon.

"Why, Mr. Satan," asked a prospective buyer, "do you ask so much for this one?" "Well," replied the old tempter, "this tool has always been my most useful. You can see that it has more wear than any of the others because I have used it to get into a person's mind to defeat him. I have relied on it when all other means failed."

Many "D" words in our normal vocabulary are adversaries to the spirit: Despair, deceit, doubt, depression, discontent, denial. . . . However, discouragement precedes the bigger, rulier weapons and is significantly used as a decoy for athletic infantry. When discouragement situates itself in a particular place, the effect can mimic a "silencer" gun.

Without the keeper's awareness, discouragement quietly passes by security checkpoints. While all military attention is paid to the more rowdy missiles of doubt and hand grenades of despair, it camouflages itself behind the Enemy's fatigues! It seems discouragement is merely a lightweight weapon in comparison! Ah . . . there's the telling evidence of its power.

In fact, the major weapon of the Enemy *is* his "costume" masking his hidden agenda. Are you aware that while the artillery unit is out trying to dissolve battles, the General has already won the war? God has won the final war and the end is in sight. The unit has been hit! It is "D-Day" for the Enemy!

We who are in Christ Jesus are the winners.

A Field of Dreams

"If your vision doesn't cost you
something, it's a daydream."
~ *John Maxwell* ~

When I speak to grade school assemblies, one of the main points I emphasize is to dream and dream BIG! I often exhort them to push past any limitations or boundaries around their lofty desires. I strongly suggest they think long and hard about what they desire to do with their life. This will awaken the fact that even at their tender age how they think will matter later.

It's not too early to begin painting a picture, "a field of dreams," with all the big stuff included. For example, when I was 11 years old, as soon as my hand touched a tennis racket I knew what I wanted to do with the first portion of my life.

My first racket was a "green-stamp racket." No one in my family was athletically inclined. One day after tagging alongside my mother at the grocery store, we found out about green stamps and later checked out the Green Stamp store. That was the day I saw my racket suspended on a bracket next to the wall.

Suddenly, the grocery store had new meaning to me. With each weekly visit I would compile hundreds of tiny green stamps and lick them to books. It would take 10 full books to purchase that racket. Eventually, that racket was taken down and placed into my hands. I couldn't have beamed any brighter; I had my first racket! Watch out, world!

Who would have ever dreamed a girl that started the game with a grocery store racket would someday grace the courts of Wimbledon six times! It's time to dream . . . big.

Napoleon Hill said, "Cherish your visions and your dreams as they are the children of your soul, the blueprints of your ultimate achievements." As the famous baseball movie liner goes, "If you build it, they will come."

I think with God, *If you dream it, it can happen!*

"C . . . C . . . Co . . . Courage"

The lion in the movie "Wizard of Oz" was so timid it was difficult for him to spit out the word *C . . . Co . . . Courage.* Proverbs 18:14 states, "A man's courage can sustain his broken body, but when courage dies, what hope is left?" (*TLB*).

Courage is simply doing what we know is right despite the paralyzing fear from within. A brave individual will risk his life, but not his conscience. Mark Twain said, "Courage is resistance to fear, mastery of fear—not absence of fear."

Edwin Louis Cole wrote in his book, *Courage: A Book for Champions,* "The athlete, the farmer and the soldier all have different ways of winning. Each of them does his training, plowing or exercising in private, and they show their abilities in public."

Reverend Billy Graham stated, "Courage is contagious. When a brave man takes a stand, the spines of others are stiffened." President Andrew Jackson commented on bravery, "One man with courage makes a majority."

However, we also need to be brave enough to live with a sense of urgent joy. Eleanor Roosevelt penned, "You gain strength, courage, and confidence by every experience in which you really stop to look fear in the face."

Think of the amount of courage it took Paul, David, Ruth, Peter, Esther and Nehemiah to summon strength to step forth in faith! Next time you have a mounting difficulty ahead of you, remember how these greats overcame their difficulties by choosing "C . . . C . . . Co . . . Courage." As

Joshua 1:5-9 emphasizes, in essence, Be strong and courageous, for the Lord will never leave or forsake you!

"Courage is fear that has said its prayers."
~ *Harle Wilson Baker* ~

The Blame Game

The first individuals to play the blame game were Adam and Eve. Life's first account is chronicled in Genesis 2:15-17 and 3:11-13. They were the first to use "The devil made me do it!" in their defense.

I don't know why we are so eager to shift blame to others, because when we accept it ourselves we are then empowered to change it!

Sport is merely a reflection of society. What we do in life will, indeed, show itself on the playing field. If we are wise, we will not be quick off the starting mark to cast blame on others. Blaming stifles growth in ourselves and others, and strife rapidly accompanies, making a bad situation worse. It rarely remedies anything but causes dissension and disharmony.

When a baseball, softball, soccer or basketball player puts his fist to his chest, it signals to the team of his admission to the error. By taking full responsibility, this player eases tension, and the team centers focus forward to the next play desiring to diligently make up for it.

Elvin Hayes said, "Blame is the coward's way out." We must be about our own business and not care who gets the blame or the glory. I've observed the best don't make excuses because they are too occupied in getting themselves better!

"A man may make mistakes,
but he isn't a failure until he starts
blaming someone else."
~ John Wooden ~

"So You're the T-Shirt Lady!"

"**S**o you are the T-shirt lady! I am so glad to finally meet the person behind the shirts," the woman exuberantly exclaimed. I looked at her quizzically. She went on to relay her story regarding a medical diagnosis she had been given about a blood disease that could have been fatal. Unless she were given a transfusion from someone with her rare blood type, she would die. She had already been feeling physically depleted, and after receiving this devastating report she became deeply depressed and despondent.

Suddenly her life was in shambles. She was filled with confusion and doubt about God's apparent lack of movement in her life. However, as the days unfolded, she would behold how intricately God would move on her behalf.

She had been participating in a fall festival when words from a T-shirt popped up directly in front of her. These words were written in big, bold, black letters: **"FOR WITH GOD NOTHING SHALL BE IMPOSSIBLE"** (Luke 1:37, KJV). She stared at the shirt for a few minutes as the words began to sink into her thoughts. Immediately she went back to her car and looked up the Scripture verse.

A few days later, she attended a baseball game. While watching the game, her attention was diverted to a boy on the sidelines. She was particularly amused with this boy because he was wearing an extra long T-shirt that hung to his knees. As the boy turned around, she saw the words again, **"FOR WITH GOD NOTHING SHALL BE IMPOSSIBLE."**

Being a Christian, she had read and heard these words before, but this time was different. She repeated the words to herself, and it struck her that God's healing was a possibility. Like a fountain, belief began to spring up within her. Soon afterward, God began to loose miracles in her life.

She was forced to undergo a hysterectomy because she was losing a great volume of blood. The combination of her blood loss, the disease, and her rare blood type dictated an emergency situation. Her father had been selected to give his blood to her, but he was out of town the day she desperately needed a transfusion.

Meanwhile, an anonymous person was strongly impressed to drop by a Blood Assurance facility to donate blood. However, their policy stated they could not see anyone without a previous appointment. For some reason, they made an exception and stayed open after hours for this individual. This person's platelets were identified as matching her blood type. It was rushed to where she was being wheeled through the hospital unit. As she received this blood, it slowly renewed her body. The healing process had begun.

We never know how or what God will use to further His promises. If He can use a donkey, He surely can use a T-shirt! When she concluded her story, I was challenged never to take lightly what God had charged me to accomplish. One of my responsibilities as the women's tennis coach at Lee University is to conduct a summer tennis clinic for kids. At the beginning of the clinic members of the tennis team disperse free T-shirts which reflect that year's theme. At the end of the clinic, the streets and stores of our city are inundated with hundreds of T-shirt laden kids. With the privilege of using sport as a medium to reach kids for the gospel, the theme of that year was **"FOR WITH GOD NOTHING SHALL BE IMPOSSIBLE."**

For with God
nothing shall
be impossible.
Luke 1:37

*Kay loving on
kids at her
tennis clinics.*

The Expectant Mother

She loved Johnny. He was her firstborn and he was well-behaved, eager to please, and sweet. As the years passed, Johnny continued to be a boy who needed no extra discipline. To prevent or correct a problem, all she did was give him a slight "I wouldn't do that if I were you" look. Johnny quickly responded and quietly found something else to do.

When Johnny was in high school, he began to deviate from this pattern of behavior. He hung out with the wrong crowd, drank alcohol, and smashed the family car numerous times. This greatly worried his mom. Yet she viewed Johnny as a compassionate and sensitive young man. She constantly set before her heart a picture of a God-fearing person. When possible, she ignored his wild tendencies and set a precedent of expectations to encourage him to believe in himself as she did. Johnny finished high school and ventured to a big university where he quickly made the dean's list. However, he became disillusioned with the prospect of becoming an engineer. He did not understand his place in the world nor his place with God. Therefore, Johnny brought his mom and dad into the living room, reserved only for "serious talk" where he announced, "I want to join the Army and find myself." He realized he was not going where he hoped in life and desperately needed a change. Mom and Dad were shocked and filled with mixed emotions. Mom's heart skipped a beat as she thought, *My son is going to war!* At that time, no one would voluntarily sign up for the war in Vietnam. Yet she was proud of him for wanting to build something of his life.

Mom responded to Johnny with much wisdom, "Son, go finish the semester, bring your grades to the point where if you ever want to go back to school you can." This he did. Later, on a cold January morning, Mom drove John (he changed "Johnny" to "John" during his college years) to the Induction Center. He made her stop one block away, and she kissed him good-bye. She watched his every step as he walked up the sidewalk. Would this be the last time she would see her son alive?

Up until that point, John's success record had been limited, but things were about to change. He went through basic training and within a year became a MP (Military Policeman). As it turned out, the only individuals in his unit who were not sent to the war zone were military policemen; they were assigned duties in the U.S. He eventually apprehended AWOLs and draft dodgers and became a military detective. John found God in small Grovetown, Georgia, during his Army "experiences." This enabled him to successfully face the challenges of life with courage and confidence. Two years later, he finished his baccalaureate degree and completed a master's degree (with a 4.0 GPA!).

John is now manager of The Mental Health Center for the state of Louisiana. He has four grown and delightful children who adore him. Romans 4:17 denotes that God who gives life to the dead [also] calls things that are not, as though they were. A mother's expectations of her son came to pass . . . and then some.

Johnny! (my brother)

Serve Him Up!

I was so excited! I had just won an event on the Women's Professional Tour—a feat difficult to come by with the likes of Steffi Graf, Martina Navratilova, and Chris Evert dominating the game! I ended my career on a good note—an ace. Um . . . of course, there was no one on the other side of the net!

The Reason for the Event: To crown "The World's Fastest Serve in Women's Tennis"

The Prize: The Concorde Award (to fly the winner anywhere in the world)

The Place: The Ericsson Championships in Key Biscayne, FL (men's and women's "6th grand slam" event)

The Stage: Center Court. Policemen with radar guns lined the court measuring the results of each hit. Yes, the competitors were sluggin' it out! Some of the finest tennis players in the world were lined along court to see who "had it"—much like the NBA Slam Dunk contest where players from around the league come together to see who can place a perfectly timed shot on demand.

My fastest serve that day in 1986 was 105 mph—the fastest in the event. British Airways gave me a sleek model of the Concorde with a ticket to fly anywhere in the world. What fun it was that day to serve my best.

Not long after that, I retired from the sport. I walked away from tennis happy and satisfied, for I had given my heart to Jesus Christ. I was ready to begin a different kind of serving. I was eager to serve on The King's Court.

As a professional athlete, my strength was my serve. I was an aggressive net player with little patience for the 50 shot rallies required in a baseline game. I simply liked to muster all my power into my serve, sprint to the net, scramble to hit a few volleys, and be done with it—next point. Better yet were the rare moments when all I did was serve and no return came back at me.

Now my favorite pleasure in life is to serve God. WOW! What fun! In this court of life I look to place myself where I can serve and expect no returns. Just go to the line (see an individual in need) and hit the ball (meet the need). Then prepare to play the next point (find another need.)

Christ came to earth to serve—not to be served. It's our turn now; it's time to serve the kingdom of God.

As Christians, it doesn't get any better than serving God. What a privilege! The eternal award goes to those who faithfully, quietly, humbly serve to the end.

This event isn't for a select few nor is it a single event. It takes all of us. So let's go serve Him up!

> "If you want to become the greatest in your field,
> equip yourself to render greater service
> than anyone else."

Kay serving in a tournament a week before the U.S. Open.

Take What's in Your Hand and Use It

Whether it is a rod, racket or slingshot, take what has been given to you and press forward. God will sustain, provide, and instill strength to overcome as you take the weapon in your hand and use it for the glory of God.

The French Open is a grueling two-week tennis tournament played on a slow, grimy clay surface that encases long grueling swings that deplete the reservoirs of the world's most outstanding physical specimens.

In the round of 16, the draw pitted the infamous three-time French Open winner Ivan Lendl against newcomer Michael Chang. Lendl and Martina Navratilova, originally from Czechoslovakia, were known for reshaping the game through their arduous conditioning practices. Meanwhile, Chang was building a reputation with his small quick steps and big heart.

Michael was down two sets to none against the great Ivan. Chang was mounting a comeback when his strength gave way. His legs felt lead-heavy and soon tightened, cramping Michael's body.

Chang could not fight anymore, so he did what he knew to do: he served underhanded! Underhanded? Wasn't that an "underhanded" thing to do? Is such a serve legal? No one had ever seen a professional start a point this way; it wasn't sophisticated, normal or pretty. This was an amateur tactic. Did Michael not realize the significance of the moment? It would be penned in tennis history books for all to read and see on television all over the world. Also, the stadium was full of people who paid good money to see grandiose tennis displays. What was he doing?

Michael served the ball underhanded, much like David took his slingshot out of his back pocket and did what seemed right to him at the moment. It wasn't the conventional way to battle;

but the old armor did not fit these young men. Both relied on what seemed unorthodox and dreadfully ordinary. Michael not only won that point but also fought four more hours to victory. He later collapsed from exhaustion in the training room.

Chang recovered and made his way to the finals of the French Open. Again, Chang fell behind two sets to one but fended off 10 break points in the fourth set and finally the decisive fifth set. Michael Chang, a 17-year-old David among tennis Goliaths, won the French Open and became the youngest—ever male Grand Slam singles champion.

He is the first to note that he won the championship with persistent belief in God. Chang, like David, relied on God to help him overcome obstacles. He pressed forward by pressing inward. God took it from there.

What has God placed in your hands?

Michael Chang at the French Open.

Friends, What's in Your Hands?

Mothers-to-be, you may not have a child in your hands yet, but you can volunteer time by holding and nurturing AIDS babies.

Fathers-to-be, you may not be playing catch with your son, but the boys club or big brother/little sister programs are desperate for attention to their kids.

Preachers, you might not be housed in a building with a steeple and have your own congregation, but the whole world is your church.

Engineers, you might not be drawing Trump Towers for profit; but your hands could construct an inner—city housing development.

Aspiring **lawyers,** you don't have a mallet to practice law, but you can go to a local courthouse and try your hand at overloaded and needy cases.

Coaches, before you have the privilege of your own team of kids to inspire, your city has a playground just waiting for your personal touch to the prized Special Olympics.

Doctors and dentists, before using the scalpel in your office, try your hand in medical missions or help kids who have deformed faces through Operation Smile.

Carpenters, you may not be erecting mansions on earth, but through your handiwork in Habitat for Humanity, a mansion in heaven is being built by the Master Carpenter!

What's in Your Hands?

A baseball in my hands is worth $6.
A baseball in Mark McGuire's hands is worth
$20 million.

A basketball in my hands is worth $19.
A basketball in Michael Jordan's hands is worth
$33 million.

A tennis racket in my hands is worth $25.
A tennis racket in Pete Sampras' hands is a
Wimbledon Championship.

A golf club in my hands is worth a slice.
A golf club in Tiger Wood's hands is worth
top dollar contracts.

A rod in my hands will mop the floor or hang a drape.
A rod in Moses' hands will part
the ravenous Red Sea.

A slingshot in my hands is a kid's toy.
A slingshot in David's hands is a
warring weapon.

Two fish and five loaves of bread in my hands
are a couple of fish sandwiches.
Two fish and five loaves of bread in God's hands
feed thousands.

Nails in my hands could build a birdhouse.
Nails in Jesus Christ's hands brought salvation
to the world.

(Author Unknown)

Contact Information

If you would like additional information, contact:

Book Web site:

http://faculty.leeu.edu/~servingthemaster/